Healthy Healing Library Series

by
Linda Rector-Page,
N.D., Ph.D

Stress,
Headaches
&
Overcoming Addictions

The Healthy Healing Library Series

As affordable health care in America becomes more difficult to finance and obtain, more attention is being focused on natural therapies and healthy preventive nutrition. Over 65% of Americans now use some form of alternative health care, from vitamins to massage therapy to herbal supplements. Everyone wants and needs more information about these methods in order to make informed choices for their own health and that of their families.

Herbal medicines are especially in the forefront of modern science today because they have the proven value of ancient wisdom and a safety record of centuries..

The Healthy Healing Library Series

Copyright 1993 by Linda Rector-Page
All Rights Reserved

No part of this book may be copied or reproduced in any form without the written consent of the publisher.

ISBN: 1-884334-08-3

Published by Healthy Healing Publications, Inc.
16060 Via Este,
Sonora, Ca., 95370.

TABLE OF CONTENTS

* Stress Management — Pg. 5
* De-Stressing Things You Can Do — Pg. 7
* What About Depression? — Pg. 8
  * Herbs Are Rich In Calming Minerals — Pg. 10
* About Massage Therapy — Pg. 10

* Stress & Mental Burn-Out — Pg. 11
* Stress & Your Glands — Pg. 12
* Stress & Your Heart — Pg. 13
* Stress & Digestion — Pg. 15
* Stress & Your Immune System — Pg. 16

* Stress & Addictions — Pg. 20
  * The Nineties Addiction – Work — Pg. 22

* About Herbs & How They Work — Pg. 25

The Different Faces of Stress

Stress Management
Relaxing Your Life

Stress is the universal enemy of modern mankind. Most Americans today are running harder and harder to stay in the same place. Many people seem to be under stress most of the time, depleting energy reserves, and creating over-acid systems that never allow for relaxation. We try to get as much done as we can in as short a time as possible. Sometimes we try to do as many things as possible at the same time!

Financial obligations, job pressures, seeking work in an increasingly down-sized job market, family demands, emotional problems, health concerns, and lack of rest and leisure can overwhelm even the most stable, well-adjusted nature. While facing challenges and difficulties helps us to grow and learn, (if we didn't have problems we would be dead), **prolonged, chronic** stress places tremendous demands on the body and mind. Everyone is affected by varying degrees of stress. At best, stress causes useless fatigue; at worst, it is dangerous to health.

Stress is our physical and emotional response to the demands of life. The key to health is how we respond to stress.

Other than an inherited propensity, stress is usually at the heart of heart disease. It is a major cause of headaches, hypoglycemia, arthritis, reduced immune response and some cancers. Indeed, most degenerative diseases are stress related. Stress irritates the body in the form of gastritis, ulcers and colitis. It irritates the mind in the form of moodiness, burn-out, overuse of drugs, depression and anxiety. Stress directly depletes the adrenal glands. In prolonged cases, the adrenals cannot raise blood sugar when necessary and hypoglycemia results. In severe cases, such as Addison's disease, the adrenals enlarge to the point of hemorrhaging and tissue death results. Stress affects the reproductive organs, libido and sexual ability. It leads to irritable bladder, acne, eczema, psoriasis, nervous tics, muscle spasms, high cholesterol, and even to baldness.

Emotions are also a key factor in stress. The inability to express emotion, loneliness, sadness, grief, and chronic depression can be just as damaging to health because they affect immune response.

Coping With Stress

Stressful situations probably aren't going to go away. So how can we handle them better?
The human body is designed to handle stressful situations. Since we thrive and are challenged by some of them, the goal ahould not be to avoid all stress, but to maintain a high degree of health and survive stress well. Poor health cannot be blamed on stress. We fall prey to stress **because** of poor health.

Controlling chronic stress often requires reorganization of lifestyle. Major problems usually require major change.

Nutrition has a major impact on how stress affects each individual. Stress depletes excessive amounts of nutrients in the body. These need to be replaced. During periods of intense stress, nutritional needs are greatly intensified. Prolonged nutritional deficiencies compound stress effects. Nutritional support is far better for dealing with stress than drugs, sedatives or chemical anti-depressants.
🍃 Eliminate sugar, caffeine and processed foods for better biochemical balance.
🍃 Add vegetable protein and mineral-rich foods, such as soy foods, sea foods, and sprouts to your diet.
🍃 Supplement your diet with B vitamins, calcium, magnesium and potassium to nourish your nerves and minimize stress.

Herbs are wonderful medicinals for overcoming stress naturally. They are rich in replacement minerals, trace minerals, and plant enzymes. They provide inner strength with bio-active, stabilizing amino acids and electrolytes that help restore body and mind energy. They correct nutrient deficiencies with vitamin B complex, vitamin C and bioflavonoids that fortify you for inner calm when the going gets tough. Sometimes you can even expect miracles.

The most popular, effective herbal combination we know to reduce stress and tension helps by repairing damaged nerve sheathing. It is a powerful nervine that quiets and soothes the brain without the addictive side effects of valium compounds. It supports healthy nerve structure, and provides a soothing influence on the brain. It promotes stabilizing body balance during high stress times. It particularly helps control acid-produced stress and emotional anxiety. It works rapidly, often within 30 minutes. It may be taken alone, or along with other healing programs to allow the body to heal itself faster and easier. The capsule formula looks like this:
BLACK COHOSH, CULTIVATED LADY SLIPPER, SCULLCAP, KAVA KAVA, BLACK HAW, HOPS, VALERIAN RT., EUROPEAN MISTLETOE, WOOD BETONY, OATSTRAW, LOBELIA.

The Different Faces of Stress

A relaxing tea to combat stress headaches, nerves and fatigue soothes the mind and restores mental energy. It may be taken anytime for a nice mental pick-me-up.
LEMON BALM, LEMON GRASS, SPEARMINT, LICORICE RT., ROSEMARY, PASSION FLOWER, YERBA SANTA, ORANGE PEEL, CINNAMON, ROSEBUDS.

Environmental conditions such as chemicals and pollutants in our food, air and water also stress our bodies and add to feelings of anxiety. Minimize your exposure to pollution. I know a good job is hard to find, but if your work place is unhealthy because of pollutants, there are many things you can do, from getting your company to take healthy precautions to wearing a dust mask. Reduce the use of strong chemicals, pesticides and solvents in your home.

Other De-Stressing things you can do:

⊃ Put your life in perspective - learn not to overreact, or take things too personally. Develop a sense of humor about life's little surprises - see them as an opportunity instead of a curse.
Shifting away from having "things" rule your life is a good move.

⊃ Learn some time management techniques. Delegate more, say no when demands from others or yourself aren't realistic.

⊃ Take a short get-away vacation. Even a long week-end in the beauty if nature can do wonders to change outlook, emotions and body chemistry.
You have to unwind before you can unleash.

⊃ Take an alternating hot and cold "hydrotherapy" shower to stimulate circulation and clear your head. This is especially good at the end of a hard work day, before you go out in the evening. I have done this many times, and you might be surprised at how your attitude and mood will change.

⊃ Get a massage - full or partial, self-given or by another, to stimulate oxygen uptake and blood flow.

⊃ Meditation is a massage for the mind. It takes practice, but can bring stillness to chaotic thoughts.

⊃ Get a little help from your friends. Just by listening, they can help

Coping With Stress

you get through tough times. Nourish your friendships. People with supporting friends handle stress much better than those who rely only on themselves.

◯ Get some aerobic exercise and fresh air 3 to 4 days a week, to increase nutrition, tissue oxygen levels and body balance. Exercise reduces muscle tension as much as 25%, and reduces anxiety for up to 2 hours after each exercise session. Diaphragmatic breathing, (like taking a deep breath before a hard task) is especially good for mental equilibrium.
Get some early morning sunlight on the body every day possible.

Depression can make you sick. Can alternative therapies help when there is severe emotional stress or chronic depression?

Chronic depression is a serious, life-limiting, immune-suppressing state that disrupts the lives of **more than 30 million Americans.** Eighty percent of terminal cancer patients have a history of chronic depression. The mental and emotional state that we call depression can stem from a wide range of causes. In general, there seem to be five broad origins for depression. 1) Great loss, as of a spouse or child, and the inability to mourn or express grief. 2) Bottled-up anger and aggression turned inward. 3) Behavior, often learned as a child, that gets desired attention or controls relationships. 4) Biochemical imbalance characterized by amino acid and other nutrient deficiencies. 5) Drug-induced depression from alcohol, sugars or prescription drugs.

> **When there is no apparent neurotic or psychotic basis for depression, nutritional and massage therapy can be far more beneficial than years of psychiatric treatment.**

The Different Faces of Stress

Severe stress weakens and imbalances the nervous system, leading to anxiety or depression. Herbal formulas can specifically help with nervous system stress support.

Herbs that have traditionally been used to lift depression include St. John's wort, rosemary, lavender, damiana and gotu kola. Herbs help restore the body's homeostasis when it is assaulted by stress. Herbal combinations are designed to address many aspects of stress symptoms.

✻ The herbal extract below is strong enough to deal with severe symptoms, yet calming, soothing and restorative. It is one of the most effective fomulas available in relieving nerve pain and muscle constriction. It helps the adrenals respond to stress by increasing the utilization of ascorbic acid stores. It aids repair of nerve sheathing. It uses rich herbal minerals to control acid-produced stress.
BLACK COHOSH, WOOD BETONY, BLACK HAW, KAVA KAVA, SCULLCAP, CARROT CALCIUM.

✻ The following herbal tea is calming and soothing to the nerves. It is particularly effective for tension head, neck and shoulder aches.
CATNIP, ROSEMARY, CHAMOMILE, PEPPERMINT, WHITE WILLOW, GOTU KOLA, FEVERFEW, BLUE VIOLET, WOOD BETONY, BLESSED THISTLE.

✻ For a measure of calm during grief, anxiety, or unidentifiable lingering depression, the following formula provides tranquility for nervous tension and severe headaches. Results are noticed almost immediately and are reported to be cumulative against depression. It is particularly helpful in re-balancing and rebuilding the nervous system and restoring mental tranquility after severe stress.
SCULLCAP, CULTIVATED LADY SLIPPER, ROSEMARY LF., CATNIP, VALERIAN, PEPPERMINT, HOPS, WOOD BETONY, CELERY SEED, CINNAMON.

✻ Long-standing depression usually involves allergies. Eliminate foods to which you are allergic. Eliminate sugars and refined foods from your diet. Avoid foods with chemical preservatives and flavorings. Avoid addicting stimulants like caffeine, alcohol and tobacco.
　○**Add 5000mg of vitamin C to your daily diet.**
　○**Add DLPA, an amino acid that increases neurotransmittors, and acts as a mood elevating supplement without the side effects of anti-depressant drugs.**
　○**Add an essential fatty acid source, such as EVENING PRIMROSE OIL to your daily diet.**

Coping With Stress

Herbs are rich sources of calming minerals

✱ **VALERIAN/WILD LETTUCE EXTRACT** includes highly absorbable sources of naturally-occurring calcium and magnesium. These herbs are synergistic as muscle relaxants for nervous tension and restful sleep. They are especially helpful for restless, hyperactive children. It may be used before retiring by both children and adults (see child dosage on page 28) to calm nerves and ease restlessness.
✱ Calcium and magnesium are nature's primary mineral elements for calming and stabilizing the body. The following herb source mineral combination is also rich in organic silica for bone, tissue and collagen formation, and for hair and nail strength.
WATERCRESS, OATSTRAW, DANDELION LEAF, ALFALFA LF., ROSEMARY, BORAGE SEED, PAU DE ARCO, CARROT CALCIUM.

✱ A hot seaweed, mineral bath is nature's perfect body/psyche balancer. Remember how good you feel after a walk in the ocean? Seaweeds purify ocean pollutants, and they can do the same for your body. Rejuvenating effects occur when toxins are released from the body. A hot seaweed bath is like a wet-steam sauna, only better, because the kelps and sea greens balance body chemistry instead of dehydrating it. The electrolytic magnetic action of the sea plants releases excess body fluids from congested cells, and dissolves fatty wastes through the skin, replacing them with depleted minerals, especially iodine and potassium. Sea plants alkalize the body with mineral riches easily absorbed through the pores.
KELP, DULSE, BLADDERWRACK, KOMBU, SEA GRASSES, SEA PALM.

Why is massage therapy so effective?

The big problem with depression is reduced energy or fatigue. Massage therapy deals directly withe skeletal-muscular areas where tenseness shows up - the stiff neck, the tight shoulders, the aching back. During massage, constricted muscles get stretched and relaxed. This improves circulation, which increases energy and reduces anxiety.

In addition, massage therapists learn how to have a nurturing touch - long, flowing strokes that can alleviate even severe, clinical depression. In this case, more **is** better - once a week is good, twice a week is excellent if you suffer from chronic anxiety. And regularity is most important, since a tell-tale attribute of serious depression is

The Different Faces of Stress

that the feeling of well-being can't last. The actual anti-depressant effects of a half hour massage last from 3 to 36 hours, but more importantly, it re-educates the body. People who go on a regular therapeutic massage program report that massage helps their bodies "remember" what it feels like to be comfortable, relaxed and cared for. I, myself have experienced this phenomenon.

Stress shows up in mental burn-out, insomnia, and lack of alertness.

There seem to be four stages to stress symptoms.

1) losing interest in enjoyable activities, sagging at the corners of the eyes, creasing of the forehead, becoming short-tempered, bored, nervous.

2) fatigue, anger, insomnia, paranoia, sadness.

3) chronic head and neck aches, high blood pressure, upset stomach, older appearance.

4) skin disorders, kidney malfunction, susceptibility to frequent infections, asthma, heart disease, mental breakdown.

Most people under stress also have trouble getting enough sleep and rest - the very thing that can most quickly improve the body's ability to deal with stress. There is a normal daily cycle between "fight or flight" and relaxation. Chronic stress arises when the relaxation phase is missed. Latest studies show that about 15% of the American population - 36 million people receive sedative drug prescriptions every year for chronic stress symptoms. Most of these prescriptions are highly addictive benzodiazepine compounds, such as Valium (30 million prescriptions), that should be used in conjunction with psychotherapy. The same study shows that almost 50 million people regularly use over-the-counter sedatives and sleeping pills. The abusive/addictive potential of these medications is not as great, but the body builds in a certain immunity to them, so that more and more needs to be taken to get the same effect.

Coping With Stress

Herbal compounds that sedate and help rebuild the nervous system are a better choice for many people, and they do not have the serious side effects or addictive potential.
Herbs can be as effective as prescription tranquilizer drugs in controlling stress, especially when used before retiring. They are calming, relaxing, fast-working blend to encourage sweet sleep. Since different nervine herbs act through entirely different pathways in the body, it is more effective to use them in combination than to take them alone.
Three choices for better sleep and relaxation are given below:
✻ **An extract formula:** VALERIAN RT., WILD LETTUCE, SCULLCAP, PASSION FLOWER, HOPS FLOWERS.

✻ A gentle, relaxing tea blend:
CHAMOMILE, SPEARMINT, SCULLCAP, PASSION FLWR., HOPS, ORANGE BLOSSOMS, ROSEHIPS & ROSEBUDS, LEMON GRASS, BLACKBERRY LF., CATNIP, HONEY CRYSTALS.
A capsule combination, especially effective for men, who report that it helps them remember their dreams for deeper REM sleep.
VALERIAN RT., SCULLCAP, PASSION FLOWER, KAVA KAVA, HOPS, CARROT CRYSTALS-35MG., GABA-30MG., TAURINE-25MG., VIT. B$_6$ -25MG., NIACIN-15MG.

Stress affects the glands at the deepest levels of the body processes.
The two most stress-involved glands are the adrenals and the thyroid.

The adrenals are composed of two parts: the cortex, responsible for cortisone production, and the medulla, which secretes adrenaline. Adrenal cortex helps maintain body balance, regulates carbohydrate and sugar metabolism, dysfunctions that result in diabetes or hypoglycemia and other stress-related diseases. The medulla epinephrine (adrenaline) and norepinaphrine speed up metabolism to cope with stress by warding off its negative effects.
Once again, while the adrenals function to help the body handle stressful situations, chronic stress exhausts them, especially when the normal body relaxation cycle keeps getting missed. (See previous page.) Nourishing stress-depleted adrenal glands is one of the primary actions to take in combatting fatigue and low energy. Herbs can supply nutrients to stimulate and nourish exhausted ad-

The Different Faces of Stress

renals so that cortical production and energy can be restored. They offer adrenal support without adding stimulants or raw animal glandular tissue. Two effective examples are given below:
the first, an extract formula, has proven more useful for men:
❈**LICORICE, BLADDERWRACK, SARSAPARILLA RT., IRISH MOSS.**
The second is a capsule combination, more useful for women:
❈**LICORICE RT., SARSAPARILLA, BLADDERWRACK, IRISH MOSS, UVA URSI, ASTRAGALUS, ROSE HIPS VITAMIN C, GINGER RT., CAPSICUM, PANTOTHENIC ACID-30MG. VITAMIN B$_6$ -15MG., BETAINE HCL-20MG.**

Thyroid malfunctions could be responsible for up to 15% of all depression cases. In most cases, a synthetic thyroid hormone is prescribed, but it may have uneven reactions and side effects. An herbal formula for thyroid health usually relies on sea plants as a gentle, safe source of iodine. The thyroid then uses them to perform its own "balancing act", raising or reducing its output as needed. An effective "iodine therapy" combination might look like this:
❈**KELP, KOMBU, DULSE, ALFALFA, WATERCRESS, BORAGE, IRISH MOSS, SPIRULINA, NETTLES.**

STRESS & YOUR HEART
Stress constricts the arterial system, creating greater circulatory disease risk.

The price for years of stress can be high blood pressure, cardiovascular disease, and congestive heart failure, along with myriad other problems. The medical profession extimates that up to 90% of all visits are stress-related.
In our experience, herbal combinations along with important diet and lifestyle improvements can make a major difference to your heart health and your life expectancy.

❧ Did you know that you can carve out health with your own knife and fork? Or that almost all circulatory diseases can be treated and prevented with diet and nutrition improvement? We all know that refined, high fat, high calorie foods create cardiovascular problems, but did you know that a natural foods diet will relieve them? Fried foods, salty foods, sugar, low fiber foods, pasteurized dairy products, red meats and processed meats, tobacco, hard liquor and caffeine are all hard on your heart and arteries. A diet that emphasizes

Coping With Stress

fresh and whole fiber foods, high mineral foods with lots of potassium and magnesium, oxygen-rich foods from green vegetables, sprouts and wheat germ (wheat germ oil can raise the oxygen level of the heart as much as 30%), and vegetable proteins brings high rewards - a longer, healthier life - and control of your life.

Circulatory problems of high blood pressure, irregular heartbeat and congestive heart failure are tied to stress reactions. Herbal formulas can address each of these problems well.

❣ An effective, fast-working combination to reduce high blood pressure tones and stimulates the entire arterial and venous structure. The formula is based on garlic, hawthorne and Siberian ginseng, three well-known, clinically proven heart and circulatory tonics. The herbs are rich in flavonoids to support better vein and capillary integrity, with gentle stimulants to increase circulatory flow. The formula includes mild herbal diuretics to keep the body from retaining fluid. It looks like this:
GARLIC, HAWTHORNE LF., BRY, & FLR., SIBERIAN GINSENG, BILBERRY, CAPSICUM, GINGER RT., PARSLEY RT., DANDELION RT., GOLDEN SEAL RT., VIT. B$_6$-15MG.

❣ A formula for congestive heart failure will help clear occlusions, stabilize the heart beat, strengthen arterial structure, reduce excess fluid, and increase anti-oxidant and free radical scavenging activity. The one below is especially effective for cardio-pulmonary conditions where there is shortness of breath. It should be used for one to three months.
HAWTHORNE LF. AND FLWR., SIBERIAN GINSENG, GINKGO BILOBA, ASTRAGALUS, COQ10-30MG., PORIA COCOS MUSHROOM, UVA URSI, CITRUS BIOFLAVONOIDS -100MG., VIT. E-30MG.

❣ The combination below is particularly beneficial for women who have entered menopause and feel that they are more at risk for stress-related heart problems. It noticeably invigorates blood circulation throughout the body, tones the heart muscle, guards against fibrillation or palpitations by regulating heartbeat, and helps prevent high blood pressure reactions by keeping the arterial/venous structure toned and elastic. We have heard many reports from women that it gives them an overall feeling of well being.
HAWTHORNE LF., BRY. & FLOWER, SIBERIAN GINSENG, MOTHERWORT, BILBERRY, CAPSICUM, GINKGO BILOBA, LECITHIN, VIT. E-25IU, ASTRAGALUS, HEARTSEASE, NIACIN-15MG., CHOLINE-15MG.

The Different Faces of Stress

❣ **SIBERIAN GINSENG EXTRACT** - as a single herb is a superior adaptogen that increases energy, reduces stress and combats fatigue. It works through the adrenal glands to support their ability to withstand stress. It strengthens the entire circulatory system, and is a specific for reducing high blood pressure.

Stress has an equal if not more dramatic effect on digestive health than even your daily diet.

Your body tells you in a variety of unpleasant ways that you are under stress - all the way from "butterflies" in your stomach to nausea to a full-blown, bleeding ulcer. Don't let it get that far. Let herbs add their powerful enzyme therapy to your tension-fighting arsenal.

✺ The following simple, gentle tea has been used for centuries to calm a nervous stomach, sweeten the breath, and end a meal with a feeling of well-being rather than heartburn.
PEPPERMINT, PAPAYA, ROSEMARY, HIBISCUS FLOWERS.

✺ If your needs are greater, an herbal enzyme, post-meal capsule like the one below can add nutrients that can help even major digestive upsets such as those caused by a reaction to drugs. Herbal enzymes also aid digestion through acid/alkaline balance. Eating under stress means that the proper enzymes often don't come into play at the right time for the right food. The herbs in this formula combine easily with digestive juices to enhance enzyme activity.
GINGER ROOT, FENNEL SEED, VEGETABLE ACIDOPHILUS, CRAMP BARK, SPEARMINT, PEPPERMINT, CATNIP, PAPAYA, TURMERIC.

Licorice root is a specific herb that protects the digestive system from damage caused by stress, and naturally promotes healing of

Coping With Stress

both gastric and duodenal ulcers. Response toits use in clinical tests is outstanding for both chronic duodenal, and acute gastric ulcers. Rather than suppressing acid release into the stomach as most drugs do, an herbal digestive formula containing licorice encourages normal immune defenses that prevent ulcer formation. Licorice help protect a healthy mucosal lining in the intestinal tract, and may be taken as needed to sooth burning and the pain of inflammation. Used over a two to three month period, a licorice ulcer compound would be effective in rebuilding healthy tissue and providing enzyme therapy for better food use.
A capsule formula might look like this:
GOLDEN SEAL RT., SLIPPERY ELM BK., LICORICE RT., MYRRH GUM, BILBERRY, CALENDULA FLR., CAPSICUM.

Stress puts the immune system under attack

Adaptogen-based formulas help the body handle stress, renew vitality and relieve fatigue.

At the end of the day, the best way for our bodies to deal with chronic stress is to have strong immune response. Providing ourselves with the best diet possible, and following a few simple watchwords is the best defense against stress.

Some of these checkpoints include:

1) Take a high potency, concentrated, green, "superfood" twice a week. Chlorella, barley grass, spirulina, and alfalfa would all fall into this category. The composition of chlorophyll is very similar to that of human plasma, so these foods provide a "mini-transfusion" for your bloodstream.

2) Include sea vegetables, such as kelp, dulse, kombu, or wakame in your diet for their therapeutic iodine, high potassium, and sodium alginate content.

The Different Faces of Stress

3) Take a high potency lactobacillus or acidolphilus complex, for friendly gastrointestinal flora, and good food assimilation.

4) Include an anti-oxidant supplement, such as vitamin E with selenium, beta carotene, zinc, CoQ 10, pycnogenol or vitamin C to protect against free radical damage, and oxygen deficiency.
Several herbs also have strong anti-oxidant qualities: echinacea, chaparral, golden seal, Siberian ginseng, rosemary, astragalus, suma, burdock, and pau de arco.

5) Protect the thymus gland from shrinking with age by nourishing this immune organ with a raw thymus glandular supplement.

6) Aerobic exercise keeps circulation flowing and system oxygen high. Disease does not readily overrun a body where oxygen and organic minerals are high in the vital fluids.

7) The immune system is stimulated by a few minutes of early morning sunlight every day. Avoid excessive sun. Sun **burn** depresses immunity.

8) Finally, laugh a lot. Laughter lifts more than your spirits. It also boosts the immune system. Laughter decreases cortisol, an immune suppressor, allowing immune boosters to function better.

Tonic herbs are good immune boosters.

Modern immune studies in the herb world have concentrated on adaptogens - substances that put the body into a state of heightened resistance. As premier adaptogens, we have found ginsengs to be an excellent choice as immune stimulators. Ginsengs from around the world offer the widest range of revitalizing activity.
A defense-restoring tea might look like this:
🌿 **AMERICAN GINSENG (RAMOSA), KOREAN GINSENG (OPT.), AMERICAN GINSENG (ARALIA),TIENCHI (JAPANESE GINSENG), SUMA (BRAZILIAN GINSENG), ECHINACEA ANGUSTIFOLIA, ECHINACEA PURPUREA, PAU DE ARCO BARK, SIBERIAN GINSENG, PRINCE GINSENG, ASTRAGALUS BARK, ST. JOHN'S WORT, REISHI MUSHROOMS, MA HUANG, FENNEL SEED.**

An immune system stengthening drink might rely on brown rice and miso for its building blocks. The following formula balances the acid/alkaline system, regulates body fluid osmosis and electrical activity in the nervous system, and aids digestion and reg-

Coping With Stress

ularity. It is a rich chlorophyll, green vitamin source, with large amounts of plant beta-carotene, B vitamins, choline, essential fatty acids with GLA, D-GLA and linoleic acid, and octacosonal for tissue oxygen. It is a vigorous source of usable proteins and amino acids, has almost twice the amount of protein as a comparable amount of wheat germ, and of course comes without the fats and density of animal protein. It is an exceptional source of alkalizing enzymes for assimilation and digestion, and for all cell functions.

🌿 **MISO BROTH & TAMARI, SOY PROTEIN POWDER, BREWER'S YEAST, VEGETABLE ACIDOPHILUS, CRANBERRIES, DULSE, WAKAME, KOMBU, SEA PALM, ALFALFA, BARLEY GRASS, WATERCRESS, OATSTRAW, YELLOW DOCK RT., DANDELION LF., BORAGE SEED, LICORICE RT., FENNEL SEED, PAU DE ARCO, NETTLES, PARSLEY RT. & LF., RED RASPBERRY LF., HORSETAIL, SIBERIAN GINSENG, ROSEMARY.**

The following "feel great" capsule combination is an over-all body tonic to enhance daily rejuvenation and ease stress. It contains a wide range of herbal heavyweights for energy and stamina. It provides usable anti-oxidants for better immune defense, mental clarity, and a feeling of well-being. It helps clean and alkalize the blood, increases circulation, provides absorbable minerals and enzyme precursors. It may be used on a daily basis.

🌿 **SIBERIAN GINSENG, UNSPRAYED BEE POLLEN, GOTU KOLA, SARSAPARILLA RT., LICORICE, SUMA, GOLDEN SEAL RT., BARLEY GRASS, SPIRULINA, SCHIZANDRA BRY., BLACK COHOSH, GINKGO BILOBA, HAWTHORNE BERRY, LF., & FLWR., AMERICAN GINSENG ROOT, ALFALFA, KELP, WILD CHERRY BK., YEAST 500, RICE PROTEIN, CAPSICUM, CHOLINE-15MG., ZINC-15MG.**

We know that most headaches are stress-related. What natural treatments are most effective for tension headaches?

The Different Faces of Stress

Tension headaches are chronic for most people under stress. It is the most common complaint we hear. The good news is that herbal analgesics **are** effective for these headaches. In general, tension headaches stem from the pain center at the base of the brain. Herbal analgesics can address very specific body areas, so they are a good choice for the types of stress headaches pain originating in this region. They work by soothing membranes, relaxing muscles and spasms, calming the mind, and providing oxygen or warmth for relief. They allow you to think clearly, and carry on with your life, while you work on stress-reducing techniques that will address the cause of the problem. All of them allow your body full function and communication with you while it is healing.

Chemical painkilling drugs, though strong, afford relief by masking pain, or deadening certain body mechanisms so that they cannot function. Herbal pain relievers are more subtle and work at a deeper level - to relax, soothe, ease and calm the distressed area. Natural pain relievers allow you to use pain for information about your body, yet not be overwhelmed by the trauma to body and spirit that unrelieved suffering can bring.

The formulas on this page are specifically targeted to stress headaches. Pick one for your symptoms.

❀ This stress relief extract is calming, soothing, restorative, **and strong**. It is especially helpful in relieving nerve pain and muscle constriction. Improvement is often felt within 20 minutes.
BLACK COHOSH, BLACK HAW, SCULLCAP, WOOD BETONY, KAVA KAVA, CARROT CALCIUM.

❀ This blend is a medicinal for those who like the tissue relaxing warmth of a hot tea. It soothes body aches, calms nerves and relieves stress headaches.
ROSEMARY, CHAMOMILE, PEPPERMINT, VIOLET, W. BETONY, BL.THISTLE, GOTU KOLA, WHT. WILLOW, CATNIP, FEVERFEW.

❀ These capsules act as a relaxant and vaso-dilator for neural pain areas in the neck and base of the brain. They encourage better body balance by providing nerve and brain nutrients. They often work when nothing else has been successful.
VALERIAN, WILD LETTUCE, ROSEMARY, FEVERFEW, CATNIP, EUR. MISTLETOE, GENTIAN RT., LICORICE RT., DLPA-25MG.

❀ These capsules are a strong, targeted combination to address the causes of cluster headaches and certain types of chronic mi-

Coping With Stress

graines. When taken on a regular basis they may used as both a control and preventive for this type of headache.
FEVERFEW FLOWER AND LEAF, VALERIAN RT., NIACIN-50MG., WILD LETTUCE, CULT. LADY SLIPPER, GINKGO BILOBA, GOLDEN SEAL RT., CAYENNE.

This tea is for people who suffer from frequent cluster headaches. It is particularly helpful against this type of headache when taken as a hot drink. It may be used both symptomatically and as a body balancer toward prevention. It is particularly effective if taken before a cranial or spinal adjustment by a chiropractor or massage therapist.
FEVERFEW, VALERIAN RT., WILD LETTUCE, DOMESTICATED LADY SLIPPER RT., GINKGO BILOBA, NIACINAMIDE-30MG.

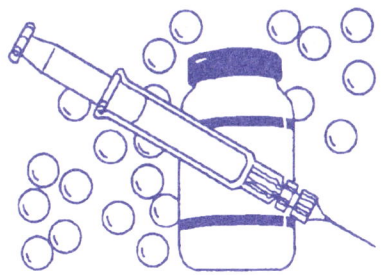

Stress & Addictions Go Hand In Hand

Drug abuse in one form or another has become a fact of modern life. American's high stress lifestyles deplete energy reserves, motivating quick "high voltage fixes" to overcome fatigue and relieve tension or boredom. Using drugs, sugar, alcohol, nicotine or caffeine as body fuel creates multiple deficiencies of vitamins, minerals, essential fatty acids, amino acids and enzymes. This depletion sets off a chain reaction which results in stress and craving for nutrients. The process keeps repeating in a futile effort to satisfy increasing need, and addiction eventually occurs.

For most people, this is just the beginning. Drug-caused malnutrition and reduced immunity swiftly lead to hypothyroidism, chronic fatigue syndrome, and auto-immune diseases such as mononucleosis, hepatitis, M.S. and AID- related syndromes. Even if these serious disorders are avoided, the consequences of drug use are high. Drug abusers and potential drug abusers are always either sick or coming down with something. As soon as one cold, sore throat,

The Different Faces of Stress

bout of "flu", or bladder infection is treated, a new one takes its place. Work is impaired, job time is lost, and family and social life is greatly affected.

Concentrated nutritional support is an essential key to recovery from addictions. The overwhelming majority of habitual addictive substance users suffer from nutrient deficiencies and metabolic or nutritional imbalances. When these conditions are corrected, the need to get high by artificial means is sharply diminished. Herbs can establish a solid foundation for rebuilding a depleted system. Give yourself plenty of time for regeneration. It often takes up to a year to detoxify and clear drugs from the bloodstream.

Herbs can help overcome addictions.
A three stage program brings the most positive results:

1) CLEANSE the body of drug residues from your body as quickly as you can. Get a cleansing massage from a good massage therapist to help normalize your system. Take a hot sauna two or three times a week; or the sweating herbal bath below:
JABORANDI, PENNYROYAL, ORANGE PEEL AND BLOSSOMS, THYME, ANGELICA RT. ELDER FLOWERS, KESU FLOWERS.

⊃Clean your lymph system with **ECHINACEA EXTRACT** drops.
⊃Clean your liver with the following liver flush tea:
DANDELION RT., WATERCRESS, YELLOW DOCK RT., PAU DE ARCO, HYSSOP, PARSLEY LF., OREGON GRAPE RT., RED SAGE, LICORICE RT., MILK THISTLE SEED, HIBISCUS.

2) STRENGTHEN your nervous system and adrenals with herbal formulas like the ones below:
🐞 For the adrenals, a combination to increase energy without adding stimulants.
LICORICE RT., SARSAPARILLA, BLADDERWRACK, IRISH MOSS, UVA URSI, ROSE HIPS, GINGER RT., CAPSICUM, ASTRAGALUS, PANTO. ACID-30MG., VITAMIN B6-15MG., BETAINE HCL-15MG.

🐞 For the nerves, a complex broad spectrum herbal nervine to help control many of the problems faced during withdrawal from drugs or alcohol. This formula is a positive factor in "getting over the hump". It is designed to depress craving, overcome nervous tension and low energy, help rebuild damaged nerve structure, encourage restful sleep, soothe withdrawal headaches, and increase attention span and focus.
SCULLCAP, SIBERIAN GINSENG, VALERIAN RT., ASCORBATE VIT. C-50MG., CHAPARRAL, KAVA KAVA, RT., WOOD BETONY, LICORICE RT., CAPSICUM, DLPA-25MG., NIACIN-20MG.

Coping With Stress

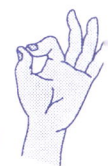

3) BALANCE your system with adaptogen/hormone balancing herbs such as the restorative formula below:
KIRIN GINSENG, CHINESE WHITE GINSENG, AMERICAN GINSENG, TIENCHI, SUMA, ECHINACEA ANGUSTIFOLIA AND PURPUREA, PAU DE ARCO BARK, SIBERIAN GINSENG, PRINCE GINSENG, ASTRAGALUS BARK, ST. JOHN'S WORT, REISHI MUSHROOM, MA HUANG, FENNEL SEED.

Most people recovering from addictions find their energy levels are very low as the body tries to carry on without its usual "high voltage fix". Herbs can help you through the energy crunch. The following high energy tea encourages better use of the body's own energy supply, and is an excellent "weaning" tea for withdrawal fatigue. It may be made up and sipped throughout the day.
GOTU KOLA, AMERICAN GINSENG ROOT FIBER, PRINCE GINSENG, DAMIANA, KAVA KAVA, RED CLOVER, RASPBERRY, PEPPERMINT, CLOVES.

Don't forget regular exercise and deep breathing during this period. These things will help keep your mind clear, your head on straight, and your body cleansed of toxins.

Work Addiction Is Becomng The Stress Hazard Of The Nineties

A major fallout of America's deficit spending eighties was that more than one member of a family had to work to keep the family at the same standard of living. If a family or individual wanted to **raise** their standard of living, they had to take on another job or extra work projects. Nineties families often have both husband and wife working two jobs, and teenage children working one or more jobs, too. It's easy to see how a workaholic lifstyle came into being and how work addiction insinuated itself into our society. Work addicts have been described as living in misery amid applause, slaps on the back, fat paychecks and performance awards.

The Different Faces of Stress

Ten signs of work addiction include:

1) A total lack of balance between work and other areas of life. Work addicts don't feel like they are worth much unless they are working. And regardless of how much they actually work, they tell themselves and everybody else that it is much more.

2) The inability to admit limitations for themselves. Consequently, they drive themselves, (and often their work associates) beyond human endurance. In addition, because of overcommitting, they hardly ever think a project through before jumping into it, or finish the project on time.

3) They judge themselves against unrealistic standards - and usually feel that nobody can do a job as well as they can. They delegate little, piling more on themselves under the guise of quality control.

4) They find it very hard to relax or have fun, feeling anxious and worthless when they aren't working. Any activity that isn't "productive" is a complete waste of time to them. They have trouble letting go of work even when they aren't physically working, and tend to tune out everything else while they plan and think about work. A bizarre side effect of this trat is that work addicts suffer "brown out amnesia" about things they did or conversations they had that weren't about work.

5) Most work addicts had strict, serious, puritanical upbringing. Consequently, they take themselves and their work very seriously with very little humor or acceptance of human frailties. The opposite side to this fact is that they are very responsible when it comes to getting a job of work done, but not very responsible at all about family commitments

6) They have a hard time with personal relationships - not only because they always have their minds on work, but because they set standards of perfection for loved ones that are impossible to meet. Work is used as shield that helps them avoid conflicts with their inner selves and their loved ones.

7) Time is the most precious commodity for a work addict. They cannot tolerate waiting, whether it be for an appointment, behind a slower car in front of them, or in a movie line. They are constantly racing against the clock. The down side is that they get there faster but lose all attention to details.

Coping With Stress

8) Work addiction is usually adrenaline addiction. So work addicts tend to turn every situation into crisis management to turn on the adrenaline high.

9) They have an enormous sense of urgency and need immediate gratification for their efforts. Most work addicts are so over-extended that their attention span is almost nil. They will rush a job through so that they can chalk up another notch on their accomplishments. The product is far more important to them than the process.

10) They are so wedded to their work that they lose the ability to make good judgements about it - work conditions, fairness, salary, advancement. Often, they become victims of the very process that they devote their lives to.

Getting unstuck from addiction to work

❀ Make a conscious effort to slow down. Stop and smell a rose or two. Learn to say no when you already have too much on your plate.

❀ Try some relaxating, stress-reducing techniques, such as yoga, meditation, daily walks, etc. The following relaxing, restoring herbal compound can help, too.
BLACK COHOSH, CULTIVATED LADY SLIPPER, SCULLCAP, KAVA KAVA, BLACK HAW, HOPS, VALERIAN RT., EUROPEAN MISTLETOE, WOOD BETONY, OATSTRAW, LOBELIA.

❀ Strengthen family ties. At the end of the day, family is what counts most. Its easy to start by celebrating a family event, tradition, or anniversary.

❀ Rekindle friendships you have let go because of work. Make some new friends. Friends are godsends of support. Caring about each other expands your interests outside of work.

❀ Develop a hobby or creative outlet you've always wanted to try.

❀ Improve your diet and get more rest. Live one day at a time.

The Different Faces of Stress

About Herbs and How They Work

What are herbs?
Herbs are concentrated foods, edible plants that are safe to take as foods, but are also rich in nutrients that can stimulate the body's healing force, and balance and regulate the human system.
1) Herbs can nourish us, especially with minerals, bolstering deficiencies from poor soil and environment.
2) Herbs can stimulate the body's healing processes by working with the system as body balancers.

Herbal combinations are not addictive or habit-forming, but they are powerful nutritional agents that should be used with common sense and care. Balance is the key to using herbal nutrients for healing. It takes a little more attention and personal responsibility than mindlessly taking a prescription drug. The results are worth it for long term health.

Even though herbs are concentrated, they are whole - not partitioned or isolated substances like drugs. Many drugs use plant isolates and concentrates, but herbs are not drugs. When dealing with chronic long standing problems, I believe the value of herbs lies in their wholeness, not in their concentration. You should not expect the same kind of activity or response that you experience from a chemically formed compound. Drugs treat the symptoms of a problem, so you generally have to take more and more of a drug to get the same effect. It is usually wise to take herbs in descending strength, always asking your body to pick up more and more of its own work.

How do herbs work?
Herbs are foundation support nutrients, working through the glands, nourishing the body's deepest elements, such as the brain, the glands and hormone secretions. Results will seem to take much longer. This is because herbs are working at the deepest levels of body balance and chemistry. **They work at the cause of the problem.** The effects are much more permanent.

However, even with slow steady action, most people feel improvement from herbal treatment in three to six days. Chronic, long standing problems will take longer. The standard rule of thumb is one month of healing for every year you have had the problem.

Coping With Stress

Herbs do not work like drugs or even like vitamins, where excess amounts flush through the body. Herbs work through the body's enzyme activity, combining with you in the same way that food does. (You are what you eat.) Herbs also contain food enzymes themselves. Their nutritional elements accumulate in the body.

I am always being asked to formulate an herbal maintenance multiple, but I don't think this would serve people well. Taking the same herbs all the time would be like eating the same foods all the time. It would lead to imbalanced nutrition from nutrients that were not in those foods.
Multiple vitamins also work best when strengthening a weak or deficient system. They are not a substitute for a balanced diet.

Herbs work better in combination than they do singly. There are several reasons for this.
1) Each formula compound contains two to five primary agent herbs that are part of the blend for specific purposes. Since all body parts, and most disease symptoms, are interrelated, it is wise to have herbs which can affect each part of the problem.
2) Body balance is encouraged by a combination of herbal nutrients, rather than a large supply of one or two focused properties. A combination gently stimulates the body as a whole.
3) A combination allows inclusion of herbs that can work at different stages of need.
4) A combination of several herbs with similar properties can increase the latitude of effectiveness, not only through a wider range of activity, but also reinforcing herbs that were picked too late or too early, or grew in adverse weather conditions.
5) No two people, or their bodies, are alike. Good response is better insured by a combination of herbs.
6) Finally, some very potent and complex herbs, such as capsicum, lobelia, sassafras, mandrake, tansy, canada snake root, wormwood, woodruff, poke root, and rue are beneficial in small amounts and as catalysts, but should not be used alone.

For more information, see "How To Be Your Own Herbal Pharmacist", a book that clearly shows people how to make and use herbal compounds for themselves, rather than to just use single herbs.

What might I experience during herbal therapy?

1) Occasionally you might experience a mild allergy type reaction as might occur in response to a food. In almost every case, this is not due to the herb itself, but to the chemicals or pesticides used in

The Different Faces of Stress

the growing or storing process; or because incompatible herbs might have been used together; or just an individual adverse reaction. The key to avoiding adverse reactions is moderation. Anything taken to excess can cause a negative side effect. Use common sense sense when taking herbs as foods or medicines.

2) As with other natural healing programs, you might experience a healing crisis during herbal treatment. This is the "law of cure" and simply means that you will seem to get worse before you get better, as the body goes through a cleansing process to eliminate toxins. Most of us can recognize this as the headache, slight nausea and weakness we feel during a cleansing fast. If there is too much discomfort, simply pace back the herbal treatment to a more comfortable level, and let it take a little longer.

How can I take herbs safely for the best results?

1) Herbs are plants for problems. Therapeutic herbs work best when used on an as-needed basis. **Herbal formulas can be quite specific for a need. Take the formula for your condition at the right time - not all the time - for best results.**
Also, rotating and alternating herbal combinations according to your health goals will allow the body to remain most responsive to their effects.

Like the rest of the natural universe, herbs seem to work better with the body when taken for six days in a row, with a rest on the seventh day.

2) Take herbs in descending strength, and rest on the seventh day each week. Start with greater amounts at the beginning of your program to build a good healing base; this starts the body's vital balancing force more quickly. As you observe your health returning, fewer and fewer of the large initial doses should be taken. At the end of the program you should be taking maintenance dosage for prevention.

For most people, they realize an herbal treatment has done its job when they forget to take it.

Coping With Stress

3) It is better to take only one or two herbal combinations at the same time. Choose the treatment that addresses your worst problem first. One of the bonuses of a natural healing program is the discovery that other problems were really complications of the worst one. They will often take care of themselves.

4) Give herbs time to work. Especially with severe, immune deficient, degenerative diseases, it takes a great deal of time to rebuild health. Patience is not an American virtue, but it is important not to add more, except under a qualified practitioner's care, even when your program is working and you can see improvement. We have found over and over again that trying to speed up benefits often only aggravates symptoms and brings worse results. Moderate amounts are excellent, mega-doses are not.
This is because the immune system is a very fragile entity, and can be overwhelmed instead of stimulated. A strong, virulent virus can even be nourished and mutate through supplementation instead of arrested by it. Give your self more time and gentler treatment. Like most other things in life, it ain't just what you do, it's also the way that you do it.

5) Herbs should not be taken like vitamins, i.e. as maintenance to shore up nutrient deficiencies. Except for some food grown vitamins, vitamins are partitioned substances. They don't combine with the body the way herbs do. Excesses are normally flushed through the system if they are not needed.
Herbs combine with the body through it's enzyme activity.

Are herbs safe for children?
Herbs are generally very safe for children. Herb dosage for children (and adults) should be based on body weight:

Child dosage is as follows:
$1/2$ dose for children 10-14 years
$1/3$ dose for children 6-10 years
$1/4$ dose for children 2-6 years
$1/8$ dose for infants and babies

A Last Word About Herbs

Science can only quantify, isolate, and assay to understand. Herbs respond to these methods, but they are so much more than a scientific breakdown. God shows his face a little in herbs. Like mankind, herbs also have an ineffable quality. Fortunately for mankind, our bodies know how to use herbs without our brains having to know why.

Booklets in the Library Series

- Renewing Female Balance
- Do You Have Blood Sugar Blues?
- A Fighting Chance For Weight Loss & Cellulite Control
- The Energy Crunch & You
- Gland & Organ Health – Taking Care
- Heart & Circulation – Controlling Blood Cholesterol
- Body Cleansing & Detoxification to Fight Disease
- Allergy Control & Management & Overcoming Asthma
- Stress, Headaches, Overcoming Addictions
- Colds & Flu & You – Building Optimum Immunity
- Fighting Infections with Herbs – Controlling STDs
- Beautiful Skin, Hair & Nails Naturally
- Don't Let Your Food Go to Waste – Enzyme Therapy
- Do You Want to Have a Baby? Natural Prenatal Care
- Menopause & Osteoporosis
- Herbal Nutrition – Vitamins, Minerals & Antioxidants from Herbs
- Herbal Therapy For Kids
- Renewing Male Health & Energy
- Cancer & AIDS – Can Alternative Therapies Help?
- "Civilization" Diseases – CFS, Candida, Lupus & More

Each of Dr. Page's written papers are thoroughly researched - through empirical observation as well as from internationally documented evidence. Studies are ongoing and updated. If you desire reference material, send a self-addressed, stamped envelope with your request to Healthy Healing Publications, 2715 Porter St., Suite 206, Soquel Ca., 95073.

BIBLIOGRAPHY

Albath, W. "Anti-Inflammatory Substances in Chamomile Oil." **Archives of Experimental Pathology and Pharmacology.** 193 (1939): 619-21.

Banerjee, B.X., and J.A. Izquierdo. "Antistress and Antifatigue Properties of Panax Ginseng: Comparison with Piracetam." **Acta Physiol. Lat. Am.** 32(4) (1982): 277-85.

Bauer, R., et al. "Immunological In Vivo Examinations of Echinacea Extracts." Arzneim-Forsch. 38 (2) 1988: 276-81.

Brekhman, I.I., and I.V. Dardymov. "New Substances of Plant Origin Which Increase Non-Specific Resistance." **Ann. Rev. Pharmacol.** 9 (1969): 419-30.

Brown, Donald J., N.D. Update on Adaptogenic Medicine: FAIM Education Fund Seminar. New York: June 20, 1992.

Foster, Steven. **Chamomile.** Austin: American Botanical Council. 1990.

---. **Echinacea: Nature's Immune Enhancer.** Rochester: Healing Arts Press, 1991.

---. **Valerian.** Austin: American Botanical Council, 1990.

Hobbs, Christopher. **Foundations of Health: The Liver & Digestive Herbal.** Capitola: Botanica Press, 1992.

Houghton, P.J. "The Biological Activity of Valerian and Related Plants." **Journal of Ethnopharmacology.** 22 (1988): 121-42.

Kim, C., et al. "Influence of Ginseng on the Stress Mechanism." **Lloydia.** 33 (1970): 43-48.

Leatherwood, P.D., et al. "Aqueous Extract of Valerian Root (Valeriana Officinalis) Improves Sleep Quality in Man." **Pharmacology, Biochemistry and Behavior.** 17 (1982): 65-71.

Mowrey, Daniel B., Ph.D. **Next Generation Herbal Medicine.** New Canaan: Keats Publishing, 1990.

Shahani, Khem M., and Custy F. Fernandez. "Anticarcinogenic and Immunological Properties of Dietary Lactobacilli." Universuty of Nebraska, Lincoln. Sept. 11, 1989.

Teeguarden, Ron. **Chinese Tonic Herbs.** New York: Japan Publications, Inc., 1985.

Wagner, H., et al. "Drugs with Adaptogenic Effects for Strengthening the Powers of Resistance." **Zeitschrift fur Phytotherapie.** 13 (1992): 42-54

Weiss, Rudolf Fritz, M.D. **Herbal Medicine.** Beaconsfield: Beaconsfield Publishing, 1988.

Zhang, Y., et al. "The Anti-Leukocytopenic and Anti-Stress Effects of Astragalus Saponins on Mice." **Nanjing Yixueyuan Xuebao.** 12 (1992): 244-8.

Each of Dr. Page's written papers are thoroughly researched - through empirical observation as well as from internationally documented evidence. Studies are ongoing and updated. If you desire reference material, send a self-addressed, stamped envelope with your request to Healthy Healing Publications, 2715 Porter St., Suite 206, Soquel Ca., 95073.

ABOUT THE AUTHOR

Linda Rector-Page has been working with nutrition and herbal medicinals both professionally and as a personal life style choice, since the early seventies. She is a certified Doctor of Naturopathy and Ph.D., with extensive experience in formulating and testing herbal combinations. She received a Doctor of Naturopathy degree from the Clayton School of Holistic Healing in 1988, and a Ph.D. in Nutritional Therapy from the American Holistic College of Nutrition in 1989. She is a licensed member of the California Naturopathic Medical Association.

She opened and operated the "Rainbow Kitchen", a natural foods restaurant, worked as an employee, and then became a working partner in The Country Store Natural Foods store. She has written three successful books in the nutritional healing field, and is founder/developer of Crystal Star Herbal Nutrition.

Ongoing contact with many manufacturers and distributors of natural products has proved very beneficial in writing her book, "HEALTHY HEALING", now in its ninth edition. In addition, Crystal Star Herbal Nutrition products, which are formulated by Linda, are carried by over two thousand natural food stores nationwide. Feedback from these direct consumer sources provides up-to-the-minute contact with the needs, desires and results being experienced by people taking more responsibility for their own health. Much of the lifestyle information and empirical observation detailed in her books comes from this direct experience. This knowledge is then translated into lifestyle therapies, and recorded in every "HEALTHY HEALING" edition.

"COOKING FOR HEALTHY HEALING", now in its second revised edition, is a companion to "HEALTHY HEALING". It draws on both the recipes from the Rainbow Kitchen and the more defined healthy lifestyle diets that she has developed from healing results since then. The book contains thirty-three separate diet programs, and over 900 healthy recipes. Every recipe has been taste-tested and time-tested as a part of each recommended diet, so that the suggested healing program can be maintained easily and deliciously with the highest nutrition.

In her latest book, "HOW TO BE YOUR OWN HERBAL PHARMACIST", Linda addesses the rising appeal of herbs and herbal healing in America. Many people have expressed interest in clearly understanding herbal formulation knowledge for themselves. This book is designed for those wishing to take more definitive responsibility for their health through individually developed herbal combinations.

Published by Healthy Healing Publications, 1993.